Introduction

According to liberal feminist thought, women have been confined to domestic roles – mothering and homemaking – and effectively excluded from important aspects of the public spheres, such as legal and governmental policy making bodies (Kaufman and Williams 2006, 1). Seeking to improve the social status and human rights of women, feminists have sought to open opportunities for women in public life, whether in politics, education, or the workforce. Although women have made substantial inroads into public life since the inception of the women's movement, beginning with First Wave Feminism in the nineteenth century, their contributions and actions are still often overlooked or trivialized by mainstream scholars and media. One of the areas in which this occurs is peacebuilding, though this also occurs in social activism in general.

Although peacebuilding often refers to activities and diplomacy at the governmental and policy level, it can also be achieved at the grassroots level. Active nonviolence is the term given for grassroots peace movements rooted in the philosophy of Mohandas K. Gandhi. He referred to this methodology as

Satyagraha, in which groups of people "withdraw their consent to be governed by those in power, using methods such as noncooperation, defiance, disobedience, refusing benefits, and creating alternatives" (Moyer 2001, 11-12). It is the methodology practiced and advocated by Dr. Martin Luther King, Jr. during the Civil Rights Movement of the 1950s and 1960s. Active nonviolence is still a framework employed in social movements today, including the ongoing peace movement and the ongoing feminist movement.

Women, in particular, are often drawn towards grassroots nonviolent actions and movements. Some theorists postulate that this is due, in part, to women's inherent "nurturing" nature. However, this is primarily due to the fact that women remain, on the average, almost completely excluded from the political and military bodies that make policy decisions, despite some exceptions. Given that women are, in general, marginalized in political decision making, some theorists postulate that grassroots active nonviolence is a natural alternative to express dissenting views and to work for social change. In fact, several examples exist of individual women and women's activist groups who advocate and employ the practice of active nonviolence. One such contemporary movement is Women in Black.

This paper seeks to explore the history and philosophy of Women in Black, both locally in Asheville and internationally. The aim is to place Women in Black within both a historical and international context, as well as situate them within feminist theory and social movement theory and to add to the growing body of scholarship on Women in Black. This is crucial, as many feminist scholars argue that women's political protests are often marginalized and/ or ignored. In order to accomplish this, the definitions of feminism, active nonviolence, and social movements will be explained and then applied to Women in Black. Given that the Asheville Women in Black group has been active since 2001, they will be given thorough consideration. This will be done using the methodologies of ethnography, participant observation, and interviewing. It is the thesis of this paper that Asheville Women in Black, as well as Women in Black internationally, serve as an seminal example of an important feminist peacemaking social movement whose methodology and strategies may be effectively applied to the conception and organization of other grassroots social movements.

Women in Black Background

Women in Black is a contemporary successful feminist and peace activist group that practices active nonviolence. Started in the late 1980s to protest the Israeli occupation of Palestine, the organization has since expanded to an internationally known and recognized activist group. It has expanded to include branches in numerous countries, including the United States, Spain, France, Italy, and Germany. Made up primarily of women, Women in Black is best known for holding silent vigils in public places in order to protest violence in all its manifestations, including war and political intimidation.

Participation is voluntary, and members need only show up at a specific time, preferably wearing black attire. Currently, the organization focuses on the wars in Iraq and Afghanistan. Inspired by earlier active nonviolence protests by women, such as Black Sash in South Africa and Madres de la Plaza de Mayo in Argentina, Women in Black subscribes to the practice of active nonviolence and serves as both an international and local example of a successful feminist peacebuilding activist group: one whose structure can serve as a template for other successful social movements. Women in Black "provided not a single model of a social movement, but a critique of freedom ... a model for discourses of women's empowerment and political action on both local and international scales" (Berkowitz 2003, 98). One scholar even notes, "...they have moved toward something like a universalizing principle for anti-militarist and anti-nuclear political organizing" (Cornell 2004, 327). Thus, analyzing Women in Black, both at the local and international level, is crucial for those interested in social activism.

Asheville Women in Black

Though Women in Black is an international movement, an active local section exists in Asheville, North Carolina. Women in Black in Asheville, North Carolina, began holding regular vigils on November 9, 2001. Their stated purpose was "to grieve for all victims of violence, including those killed in the September 11 attacks and those being killed and injured in Afghanistan by US military action; and to call for peace" (Asheville Global Report

2001). As in other Women in Black vigils around the world, Asheville Women in Black wear black, stand silently, and hold signs. "We women dress in black as an expression of grief for all the victims of violence and war. We stand in silence because mere words cannot express the tragedy that wars and hatred bring" (www.main.nc.us/wib).

This particular group was inspired to form in part due to the treatment of the San Francisco Women in Black. During 2001, San Francisco Women in Black was targeted by the Federal Bureau of Investigation, and members were called to testify in front of a Grand Jury. According to Asheville Women in Black, "In solidarity with the women who are facing Grand Jury investigation, and more importantly in determination to allow a space for mourning the dead and grieving loss of life in senseless acts of violence, women in Asheville are taking up the mantle of Women in Black" (Asheville Global Report 2001).

Asheville Women in Black remains active, holding a weekly vigil every Friday from five to six pm. at the Vance Monument in Pack Square in Asheville. Women are the ones who are explicitly invited to join the vigil.

> We invite all women to stand with us in silent reflection about ourselves and in solidarity with all who have been raped, tortured and killed. We stand for those who have been disappeared, whose homes have been demolished, whose loved ones have been maimed or murdered in violent acts, for the imprisoned, for the soldiers and for the civilians – for all those caught in the cycle of violence. Through the power of silent witness we call for its end. (www.main.nc.us/wib)

However, Asheville Women in Black also has a policy regarding men who wish to participate. As is the case with the original Women in Black, the Asheville group believes that women's voices and views are often lost in mixed gender groups. Thus, while men can offer support from the side, the vigil is primarily made up of women.

> In past vigils, empathetic men have sometimes come to stand in solidarity with us. When these allies position themselves to the side or behind our semicircle and respect the silence, we welcome the non-intrusive support. We will continue to invite only women to stand with us in our weekly vigil, yet are grateful for the solidarity of like-minded men when it is offered (www.main.nc.us/wib).

This insistence on the part of the Asheville Women in Black that the movement remain women only makes sense in light of existing and functioning within the current patriarchal paradigm.

History and Philosophy of Women in Black

Feminism and active nonviolence intersect in Women in Black. Women in Black describe themselves not as an organization but as "a means of communicating and a formula for action" (www.womeninblack.org). At the core of Women in Black is action, specifically nonviolent and non-aggressive forms of action. The most frequently used and widely known nonviolent action used by Women in Black is the vigil. Women, and men, who participate in these vigils wear black, are often silent, hold signs, and pass out literature. "In addition to vigils Women in Black groups use many other forms of non-violent direct action such as sitting down to block a road, entering military bases and other forbidden zones, refusing to comply with orders, and 'bearing witness' (www.womeninblack.org).

Dressing in black during vigils is highly symbolic. "Wearing black in some cultures signifies mourning, and feminist actions dressed in black convert women's traditional passive mourning for the dead in war into a powerful refusal of the logic of war" (www.womeninblack.org). Vigils adopt feminist structures and format: "nonhierarchical, consensus-seeking decision making, and nonviolent responses to provocation" (Svirsky 2003: 546). Though Women in Black do not possess a specific manifesto or constitution, their perspective is informed by feminist theory: "male violence against women in domestic life and [violence] in the community, in times of peace and in times of war, are interrelated" (www.womeninblack.org). Women in Black agree with feminist theorists that violence is a powerful means for controlling women. Thus, Women in Black does not explicitly exclude men; men who subscribe to feminist principles and refuse to fight are supported by Women in Black. Feminist theory also subscribes to the notion, as does Women in Black, that women experience war differently than men do:

> Women-only peace activism does not suggest that women, any more than men, are 'natural born peace-makers.' But women often inhabit different cultures from men, and are disproportionately involved in caring work. We know what justice and oppression mean, because we experience them as women. Most women have a different experience   of war from that of most men. All women in war fear rape. Women are the majority of refugees. A feminist view sees masculine cultures as specially prone to violence, and so feminist women tend to have a particular perspective on security and something unique to say about war.
> (www.womeninblack.org)

Women in Black supports the view that women only activism is as important as mixed gender activism. Women acting exclusively with other women are less likely to have their voices and views drowned out.

Women in Black supports international women's solidarity by holding international conferences and arranging cross-cultural visits and exchanges via electronic media and the internet. "WiB includes women of many ethnic and national backgrounds, co-operating across these (and other) differences in the interests of justice and peace" (www.womeninblack.org). Even though Women in Black is a worldwide movement, it is impossible to know precisely how many women have participated and/or continue to participate in feminist nonviolent actions. Women in Black does not require any specific criteria for membership or to start a vigil. "Any group of women anywhere in the world at any time may organize a Women in Black vigil against any manifestation of violence, militarism or war" (www.womeninblack.org). Indeed, instructions for beginning and holding regular vigils is part of their website. These vigils are the primary mode of communicating with the public and with each other, opening up "public discourse on the war and militarism" (Ganeshpanchan 2009, 166). Emails serve as a method of communication among members and participants outside of vigils, and Women in Black maintain a strong web presence for the purpose of communicating with the outside world (Ganeshpanchan 209, 166).

Women in Black draws from earlier women's nonviolent activism, most notably from the Black Sash movement of South Africa. These were white women who sought to fight apartheid; their trademark was a black sash worn over their clothes to protest racism (Svirsky 2003, 548-549). Women in Black also draws from the Madres de la Plaza de Mayo in Argentina, who wear white headscarves embroidered with the names of disappeared family members. Unfortunately, as is the case in much of women's history, "Most Women in Black, regardless of where they stand, know nothing of these organizations or movements, as it is still regrettably common for the history of women in the world to pass unnoticed" (Svirsky 2003, 549). Women in Black was also the first successful feminist active nonviolent group to make an impact without appealing to motherhood (Baum 2006, 564). "...Women in Black have used other images of femininity – women as mourners, dressed in black, but also just women, standing outside, claiming their right to speak about national matters as women" (Baum 2006, 565).

In Israel, Women in Black originated in 1988 as a response to the occupation of Palestine and the Palestinian Intifada:

> Israeli Jewish women began to stand in weekly vigils in public places, usually at busy road junctions. Starting in Jerusalem, the number of vigils in Israel eventually grew to almost forty. In the north of Israel, where the concentration of Arab communities is greatest, Palestinian women who are Israeli citizens were also active in Women in Black groups. Many local WIB groups made contact with women across the Green Line engaged in support work, e.g. visiting Palestinians in Israeli prisons. (www.womeninblack.org)

During the vigils, women carried signs saying "End the Occupation" and other related slogans. Vigils were always held at the same site, at the same time, and the women wore black. Though initially the vigils were not completely silent, the women did not chant. Though they faced verbal abuse, often in sexual terms, the women's policy was to not shout back; rather, they sought to maintain dignity. The vigils spread by word of mouth, and now spread by technology, "driven by the desire of women to 'do something' and inspired by the example of those who were already on a vigil" (Svirsky 2003, 545).

Women in Black's format soon caught on internationally, and groups were formed in Canada, the United States, Australia, and many European countries in order to support the original Israeli group. Italian women began Women in Black groups and vigils in 1988, drawing upon their prior history of a program of visits to Israel/Palestine. Other women's activist groups formed during the Gulf War, beginning in 1991, and eventually renamed themselves Women in Black. The format of vigils is one of the "most far-reaching contributions of Women in Black to the peace movement – it enabled women everywhere to participate" (Svirsky 2003, 545).

Women in Serbia became involved in Women in Black when war broke out in the former Yugoslavia. Women in Black in Belgrade formed on October 9, 1991. "Explicitly feminist, they have been actively opposing nationalist aggression and masculine violence ever since" (www.womeninblack.org). Women in Black in Belgrade held regular vigils in Republic Square in Belgrade and are described as having a "strong and challenging street presence" (www.womeninblack.org). They are still active, working in partnership with men who refuse military service, organizing international meetings and visits, writing and publishing, and maintaining "an extensive programme involving public statements" (www.womeninblack.org). A Spanish network of Women in Black, Mujeres de Negro, also became active around the same time. "They helped find refuge, respite and a public platform in Spain for women from the Yugoslav region" (www.womeninblack.org).

Women in Black continued to spread to other countries. During the wars in Croatia and Bosnia is 1992, a Women in Black group formed in Belgium, and Women in Black London took their name. Groups in a wide variety of countries emerged in the mid-nineties and later. "Some groups adopted the formula of silent vigils, wearing black. Others (for instance the Bay Area WIB in California and WIB in Tokyo) have found it more effective, for instance, to process in single file, silently, through shopping areas, or to use masks, giant puppets, and drums" (www.womeninblack.org). As did other Women in Black groups, these groups also made a practice of visiting war zones in support of the women there.

Women in Black in India was formed in 1992, when the Babri Masjid (an ancient mosque) was torn down by fundamentalist Hindus. Women in Black stood in silent vigil every Thursday in the city of Bangalore, in the streets, in market squares, and in the Gandhi

Peace Park. Similarly, Women in Black in the Philippines was formed in 1995 and drew upon the tradition of earlier activist groups who dressed in black and stood in front of the Japanese Embassy in Manila, demanding compensation for World War II Comfort Women. It was one of these groups, the Asian Women's Human Rights Council, that organized along with Women in Black of India to hold a massive Women in Black vigil in Beijing on September 4, 1995. This vigil, attended by some three thousand women, was planned to take place concurrently with the UN World Conference on Women. Women in Black in Nepal has held silent vigils in public places in Katmandu since 1996. Women in Black groups around the globe demonstrated against the United States' military actions in Iraq, Sudan, Afghanistan, and Belgrade in 1998 and 1999.

Women in Black in Israel became highly active again with the renewal of the Palestinian intifada in September 2000. Women began standing in six sites: Nazareth, Acre, Haifa, Tel Aviv, Jerusalem, and the Nachson junction. In November 2000, the Israel Coalition of Women for a Just Peace was formed, bringing together all Women in Black vigils as well as nine other women's peace organizations. These women, dressed in black, have carried out direct action in addition to holding vigils. In addition, Women in Black held vigils at all seventeen Courts of Women put together by The Asian Women's Human Rights Council and El Taller International, both networks of women's human rights organizations.

Women in Black intensified their nonviolent actions after September 11, 2001. Women in New York and other locations in the United States issued the statement, "Justice not vengeance" (www.womeninblack.org). Many groups also protested the "war on terror" in Afghanistan and elsewhere. In 2002, Women in Black groups began "actively opposing any extension of military action by the USA and allied governments to attacks on particular states, notably Iraq" (www.womeninblack.org). During this time, Mujeres de Negro in Spain also coordinated a worldwide action in order to protest the Colombian drug-related war. On January 4, 2003, a massive vigil was held at the Asia Social Forum in Hyderabad. Over three thousand women, dressed in black, attended for the purposes of "protesting Israel's Occupation of Palestine, the war on Iraq and the war crimes of the USA, and other situations of war and armed conflict" (www.womeninblack.org). During this time, a Canadian chapter of Women in Black was formed in Edmonton, Canada. "All of us, young and old, and from disparate histories, confessed to feelings of powerlessness in the post-September environment. But the idea of being Women in Black excited us. We would step into the circle already joined by Muslim and Jewish women in Jerusalem..." (Kostash 2003, 592). The Asheville Women in Black also came into existence after September 11, 2001.

Women in Black have been recognized both locally and internationally, receiving a number of awards for their peacework. The Millennium Women's Peace Prize was awarded to the worldwide network by the NGO International Alert and the UN agency UNIFEM. In 2001, Women in Black was nominated for the Nobel Peace Prize. Women in Black in Italy were awarded the Gold Dove of Peace, an Italian prize, in 2003, and the worldwide network was honored by Church Women United, USA. Israeli Women in Black received three awards: the Aachen Peace Prize in 1991, the peace award of the city of San Giovanni d'Asso in Italy in 1994, and the Jewish Peace Fellowship's Peacemaker Award in 2001.

Feminism Defined

Women in Black characterizes itself as a feminist movement; thus, examining feminism as it applies to Women in Black will be helpful. As with any overarching concept and/or philosophy, feminism is complex. Given that it is an ever-changing and expanding ideology, no succinct definition can ever be wholly adequate. However, according to Barbara Arneil in *Politics & Feminism*,

> a preliminary definition of feminism might be: The recognition that, virtually across time and place, men and women are unequal in the power they have, either in society or over their own lives, and the corollary belief that men and women should be equal; the belief that knowledge has been written about, by and for men, and the corollary belief that all schools of knowledge must be re-examined and understood to reveal the extent to which they ignore or distort gender. (Arneil 1999, 3-4)

Indeed, at the core of feminism theory is the understanding that women have been historically and systematically oppressed due to a distorted belief that men are inherently superior creatures, regardless of the fact that men experience power differently. In this context power is defined as the ability to influence one's personal circumstances.

The feminist movement and feminist theory seeks to correct this distortion through methodologies based on a variety of ideologies. According to Marlene Legates in *In Their Time*, "the most important theoretical distinction today with antecedents to the past is the distinction between liberal, equity, or equal-rights feminism on the one hand, and cultural feminism on the other" (LeGates 2001, 5). Liberal feminism seeks to emphasize the similarities between women and men. This is often expressed as an agenda to obtain women's legal and political rights (LeGates 2001, 5-6). Cultural feminism, conversely, emphasizes the differences between women and men. Its goal is not to pursue equality with men; rather, cultural feminists stress a "woman-centered perspective, one that emphasizes the female values and culture arising from women's unique experiences" (LeGates 2001, 6). Rather than strive for equal rights, the cultural feminists' goal is to integrate "women's values" into society (LeGates 2001, 6). Liberal feminism and cultural feminism are two poles on a richly varied continuum and are not necessarily diametrically opposed. In order to better understand the development of these poles and to place Women in Black within the context of feminism, it is necessary to briefly discuss the history of feminism in the West.

A Brief History of Feminism in the West

Feminism in the West is often separated into three distinct phases, or waves. Drawing from the liberal tradition, First Wave feminists "struggled for a formal equality for women within the existing systems of rules and laws" (LeGates 2001, 4). While loosely organized feminist networks were already in existence, First Wave feminism formally began in the 1850s and 1860s when reformers in Europe and North America formed more permanent organizations (LeGates 2001, 197). Culminating in achieving women's suffrage near the time of World War I, First Wave feminism focused primarily upon "the male monopoly of education, professional careers, and culture; married women's economic and legal dependence; sexual and moral double standards; women's lack of control over their bodies; the drudgery of housework; low wages; and, not least, women's exclusion from politics" (LeGates 2001, 197). Many of the issues that First Wave feminism tackled remained on the agenda of Second Wave feminists. Partially due to this fact,

First Wave feminists have been criticized for not achieving more than they did. Marlene LeGates gives three reasons for this perceived lack of progress: "Their 'mistakes' were, first, letting themselves become sidetracked by the suffrage campaign; second, perpetuating a conservative view of the family and women's roles that substantiated rather than subverted separate-spheres ideology; and third, failing to overcome a white, Eurocentric, middle-class orientation" (LeGates 2001, 237).

When speaking about feminism, often historians exclude the years between first and second wave feminism, a period which scholars term "Inter-War feminism" (LeGates 2001). Though this period lacked an effectively organized and highly visible feminist movement, "[f]eminists continued to articulate their concerns and press their campaigns from 1914 to the 1940s..." (LeGates 2001, 281). Feminists of this period were less successful due to at least two critical reasons. First, the end of World War I brought about a conservative backlash, and second, reformers who had focused exclusively on suffrage often left the movement (LeGates 2001, 281-282). "The years from World War I to the beginning of World War II were difficult years for feminists, indeed for reformers or radicals of any kind. Postwar political tensions, economic downturn, and the rise of fascism all made it seem reasonable to cling to what one had rather than to try for more" (LeGates 2001, 321). As a result, many feminists redirected their energies into other causes not necessarily associated with traditional First Wave feminism:

> Putting the decisive lie to the notion that women's activism ebbed during the interwar years were the international organizations that flourished during this period: namely, the International Council of Women; the International Woman Suffrage Alliance, which greatly broadened its mandate after the war; and the Women's International League for Peace and Freedom. (LeGates 2001, 197)

Given the stigma of the feminist label, these organizations and the women involved in them focused more generally on social and humanitarian concerns. In addition, interwar feminism did not necessarily seek to challenge gender roles. "There was no attempt to challenge the idea of woman in the home or to encourage women's entry into the public sphere. On the contrary, the point was to elevate women's role within the home and to protect them when necessity demanded that they work outside of it" (LeGates 2001, 300). Thus the feminist movement was alive, if not thriving.

The beginning of Second Wave feminism is often cited as beginning with Simone de Beauvoir's *The Second Sex*, originally published in 1949 (Arneil 1999, 163). She is labeled a Second Wave

feminist due to the fact that she is an existential feminist, arguing

that "if women are to be truly free they only have to make certain

choices. First, they must overcome their biology, their bodies, in

order to enter the cultural, rational realm of men; second, women

should consider seriously their continued role in the private sphere,

most specifically their role as mothers" (Arneil 1999, 163). She is

credited with being the first feminist thinker to question women's

role in the private sphere – one of the main characteristics of second

wave feminism. Other scholars point to the publication of Betty

Friedan's *The Feminine Mystique* in 1963 (LeGates 2001, 328). Her

advice to women was to seek fulfillment through work outside of the

home (LeGates 2001, 345). Regardless of the exact year, most

historians and feminist scholars point to the emergence of Second

Wave feminism in the late 1960s and early 1970s (LeGates 2001,

328).

Second Wave feminism is characterized by two main strains:

liberal, or equal rights feminism and radical feminism. Liberal or

equal rights feminism is noted for its similarity to first wave liberal

feminism. "It assumed the goal of equality between women and men but with an emphasis on combating economic as well as legal discrimination and, in addition, sexist attitudes" (LeGates 2001, 346). Radical feminism, however, pointed to patriarchy as the cause of male dominance. Unlike liberal or equal rights feminism, it "focused on the family and personal relationships rather than the world of politics or paid employment" (LeGates 2001, 346). The main slogan used by radical feminists was "the personal is political" (Arneil 1999, 166). Even the language used by the radical strain of feminism was different than the language of liberal feminism – liberation versus equality or rights, oppression rather than discrimination, and revolution in contrast to reform (LeGates 2001, 351). As such, radical feminism often was associated with hostility towards men. "Radical feminism meant breaking not only with leftist men but with Marxist ideology, which insisted on economic class as the main form of oppression" (LeGates 2001, 357). Second Wave feminism peaked in the 1970s.

Beginning in the late 1980s and continuing beyond, feminism moved into a Third Wave. Drawing upon the successes and failures of earlier feminisms, the Third Wave "began as feminists came to realize that the theoretical frameworks they had been using, built on the foundations of universality, sameness and scientific methodology, were becoming increasingly difficult to reconcile with where feminism had led them: to notions of identity, difference, particularity and embodiment" (Arneil 1999, 186). Instead of relying upon existing theoretical schools and Western dualistic though, Third Wave feminism began with the central concepts of "difference rather than sameness, identity and particularity rather than universality, celebrating the status of the other or outsiders rather than wanting inside, embodiment rather than the view from nowhere and, finally, a relational rather than binary approach" (Arneil 1999, 187). Thus, Third Wave feminism seeks to base its theoretical underpinnings on the perspectives and experiences of women rather than men (Arneil 1999, 187).

Third Wave feminist writing is characterized by specific themes. First, essays are written in narrative form in a personal and popular nature. The rationale given is that this personal type of writing is the most political and accessible. Second, Third Wave feminists recognize the "multiplicity of identity and difference among women and the difficulties in categorizing oneself" (Arneil 1999, 189). Third, Third Wave feminist writing attempts to be honest and forthcoming about the contradictions faced on a day to day basis by women. The goal of this perspective is to challenge the "perceived rigidity in the ideals of second wave feminist politics" (Arneil 1999, 189). Finally, Third Wave feminism questions feminist academia and its chosen media. In contrast to traditional academic journals, Third Wave feminists disseminate information though a variety of media, including the internet and zines (Arneil 1999, 191). Women in Black began and continues to function during the time frame of Third Wave feminism and exhibits the characteristics of a Third Wave feminist movement.

Active Nonviolence Defined

Both feminism and active nonviolence seek to address and correct inequality. Nonviolence is the theory of pacifism, but active nonviolence entails acting upon the principles of pacifism in order to enact social change. "Active nonviolence ... is behavior aimed at influencing political policy and decision making, usually through groups, whether amorphous or well structured, and through other than the standard procedures, such as voting in a political democracy" (Schwebel 2006, 197). The rationale for active nonviolence is its proven effectiveness. Nonviolence "provides social movements with the optimum opportunity for success because it's based on timeless universal human values and principles – love, compassion, cooperation, and caring" (Moyer 2001, 11). It is less threatening than other methods and thus facilitates the openness of the social movement's message to a larger audience. Active nonviolence is often compared to or equated with M. Gandhi's concept of Satyagraha.

> [Gandhi] taught that the power of social movements is based on their ability to mobilize the populace in a moral struggle in which the people withdraw their consent to be governed by those in power, using methods such as noncooperation, defiance, disobedience, refusing benefits, and creating alternatives. This moral struggle requires total nonviolence in attitude and actions towards people and property (Moyer 2001, 12).

Active nonviolent methods provide the opportunity for nearly everyone to participate in a social movement: "women, men, elders, youth, the frail, and even children, including those people who would be unable or unwilling to carry out militaristic and violent social action" (Moyer 2001, 11). Active nonviolence engages the maximum power of the people to be applied. This was demonstrated clearly by M. Gandhi. However, feminist theorists often point out the problematic nature of using M. Gandhi as a reference point for nonviolence, as "his own personal life and many of his writings are plagues with inconsistencies towards women" (Mason 2005, 741). Regardless, M. Gandhi's ideal of active nonviolence can be applied to Women in Black.

People are motivated to participate in active nonviolence because of the certainty that their deeply held beliefs are being threatened. "They have both a sense of responsibility to act and confidence that their actions will have a palpable effect" (Schwebel 2006, 197). Not all nonviolent activists choose to take part in large social movements; some choose to act on a more individual level.

> ...[P]eople can adopt active nonviolence methods of resolving conflict through means other than participation in social movements at times of crisis. Those means include education designed to stimulate realistic empathy, encourage constructive interpersonal contact between members of hostile groups, and provide experience in the use of nonviolent conflict management. (Schwebel 2006, 198)

Participants in active nonviolent action embody strong motivation, independent thinking, and a need to provide the general population with guidance, leadership, and information (Schwebel 2006, 198). Women in Black, both internationally and locally, professes to subscribe to the tenets of active nonviolence.

Characteristics of Social Movements

As Women in Black characterizes itself as a movement, it is necessary to discuss the characteristics of social movements. According to Bill Moyer in *Doing Democracy*, "[s]ocial movements are collective actions in which the populace is alerted, educated, and mobilized, sometimes over years and decades, to challenge the powerholders and the whole society to redress social problems or grievances and restore critical social values" (Moyer 2001, 10). Yet not every cause or social movement is successful in disseminating its message, receiving support from the general populace, or achieving its goals for change and awareness. Regardless, social movements play a crucial role in mobilizing the populace and effecting change. "Ordinary women and young people who speak collectively may be perennial irritants, but mobilizations are necessary to keep the channels of democratic debate open" (Kaplan 2003, 208). Indeed, Women in Black seeks to mobilize the public.

Moyer states that social movements exhibit four primary characteristics. First, they promote participatory democracy. This means they provide a role for anyone who is interested in participating, and everyone should be involved in the decision-making process. Second, social movements are situated at the center

of society; ordinary people play a crucial role in the process of

change, effectively placing successful social movements in society's

mainstream. Third, social movements are necessarily based upon

widely held universal values:

> To place their social movement in the center of society, gain
> the support of the majority of the public, and advance society
> along the path of human development, movement activists
> must consciously stand for and articulate the culture's
> fundamental values, such as justice, democracy, civil and
> human rights, security, and freedom. (Moyer 2001, 11)

Most citizens believe strongly in such values, and thus successful

social movements effectively present a truer embodiment of these

values than that presented and practiced by those in power. Fourth,

social movements must employ nonviolent methods because they are

incredibly powerful. Women in Black possesses all four of Moyer's

social movement characteristics.

In any social movement, including that undertaken by

Women in Black, specific participant roles exist. According to

Moyer, social movement activists can be divided into four roles: the

citizen, the rebel, the change agent, and the reformer. Each role

serves a distinct function and can be used both effectively and ineffectively. In fact, all social movements require all four roles in order to be effective (Moyer 2001, 21). In general, the citizen role applies to the majority of the populace in any given country. In an activist role, citizens promote positive values, principles, and symbols as well as promote an "active citizen-based society where citizens act with disinterest to assure the common good" (Moyer 2001, 28). The rebel is often more visible in a social movement. Rebels in general tend to be courageous, exciting, risky, and fond of public attention. Effective rebels function to put issues and policies in the public spotlight and engage in protest; they often partake in nonviolent, direct actions such as demonstrations, marches, rallies, and acts of civil disobedience. In the case of Women in Black, vigils are the primary method of nonviolent, direct action.

Reformers function as watchdogs who work to assure the enforcement and expansion of successes as well as protect against backlash. The reformer's goal is to get the movement's values and goals adopted into policy and law using a variety of means, such as lawsuits, referenda, rallies, and lobbying. Change agents work to educate and involve the majority of citizens and society on issues. They seek to create and support grassroots organizations and activism and promote strategies and tactics for the long term by involving per-existing grassroots organizations, coalitions, activists, and networks (Moyer 2001, 29). Though Women in Black participants are most effectively classified as rebels, the movement itself does seek to draw in citizens and engage the attention of change agents and reformers.

While Moyer writes about social movements in general, West and Blumberg in *Women and Social Protest* focus particularly on women's social movements, classifying them into four categories:

1. Those directly linked to economic survival
2. Those related to nationalist and racial/ethnic struggles
3. Those addressing broad humanistic/nurturing problems
4. Those identified in different eras as "women's rights" issues (West and Blumberg 1990: 13).

It is crucial to discuss feminist theory regarding social movements and nonviolence, as "...women activists have frequently left the nonviolence movement, since it directly conflicted with their commitments to feminism" (Mason 2005, 740). As Women in Black primarily focuses on mourning and calling attention to violence, they fit best within West and Blumberg's third category. However, it is arguable that Women in Black may overlap into the second category, as well. This is due to the original purpose of Women in Black: to oppose the Occupation of Palestine and the Intifada. This is clearly a nationalistic struggle as well as a racial and ethnic one.

Social movements, including Women in Black, progress through a series of stages, yet not every social movement lasts long enough to progress through all eight stages outlined by Moyer. The first stage of a social movements is termed "Normal Times." During this stage of social movements, a critical social problem is identified that violates widely held beliefs; however, the majority of the public is unaware of the social problem. During the second stage, called "Proving the Failure of Official Institutions," the purpose is to prove the failure of official institutions and policies. At this time, activists work to become experts on the issue by doing research, and, as a result, new local opposition groups are formed. The third stage is called "Ripening Conditions." During this stage, recognition of the problem grows, and approximately twenty to thirty percent of the general public opposes the policies of the powerholders (Moyer 2001, 44-45).

The fourth stage is termed "Take Off." This is precipitated by a trigger event and is characterized by dramatic nonviolent campaigns and actions. Nonviolent actions are repeated nationally; the purpose of these actions is to show the public that the current conditions and policies actually do violate widely held values. The repetition creates visibility; visibility fosters awareness. During the fifth stage, "Perception of Failure," activists often perceive that they have not achieved their goals because numbers are down at demonstrations and the powerholders' actions appear unchanged; common feelings for activists are despair and hopelessness. The movement may then progress onto the sixth stage: "Majority Public Opinion," in which the majority of the population opposes the present policies and conditions. However, the powerholders may still seek to promote the public's fear of activism and alternatives. The seventh stage, "The Success Stage," is characterized by a large majority of the population opposing current policies and no longer fearing the alternatives. During this stage, the powerholders who do not change policies are often voted out of office. The eighth, and final, stage is "Continuing the Struggle." Activists try to extend their successes while opposing backlash attempts; the movement continues to promote a paradigm shift and focuses on other sub-issues (Moyer 2001, 44-45). The success, or effectiveness, of social movements is nearly impossible to quantify, as both of these are ambiguous terms. However, according to Kaplan in *Taking Back the Streets,* "Mobilizations and other forms of direct action did not themselves bring down the authoritarian regimes, but they weakened them" (Kaplan 2003, 206). Although she is speaking specifically in regards to grassroots activism in Chile, her point is clear. Grassroots social movements are key to social change and cannot be ignored. Thus, Women in Black must be examined.

Women's Nonviolent Activism

As stated earlier, Women in Black is a feminist nonviolent social movement; thus, Women in Black enables us to examine how and why women's nonviolent activism differs from that of men's. Although women's peace activism is often more prevalent than that of men's, it is often less visible or marginalized. Although women and children make up seventy-five percent of people displaced due to war and are instrumental in rebuilding areas after war, they are not as involved in the peacebuilding process as men are (Myers 2001, 7). Regardless, many feminist and women's groups for peace pre-date Women in Black, including: Women's Strike for Peace, Women's

Peace Society, Women's Peace Union, The Women's Peace Party, Women's International League for Peace and Freedom, and National Committee for the Cause and Cure of War (Myers 11.16.2009). Perhaps one of the most widely known contemporary groups is Code Pink, which originated in the United States in order to protest the invasion of Iraq.

Unfortunately, women and women activists are often excluded from the political and decision making process; although women may advocate diplomacy and/or negotiations, they are often dismissed (Anderlini 2007, 36). This is not to say that women have not held or do not hold some political power. Regardless, few have been leaders of state. "Such women, however, are often regarded as unusual in a world of power, high stakes, threats, and war. Such an environment is said to be a man's world, and these women are doing a 'man's job'" (Beckman and D'Amico 1994, 1). Tragically, women also often face violence, ostracism, and/or sexual violence when speaking out or advocating in a way that is seen as in conflict with "traditional" gender roles. Thus many women's activist groups and women activists seek not only to challenge violence and war, but also to target oppression and injustice. "Women's mobilization efforts often commence with a focus on issues, with a view to

influencing changes within the political leadership" (Anderlini 2007,

36). Regardless, the goal is not necessarily to dismantle entire

political structures or to challenge the existence of states. Rather,

women's activist groups seek to find and advocate an alternative

paradigm – one in which issues and conflicts that could lead to

violence are confronted.

> The vision of such groups – increasingly found around the world, often led or supported heavily by women, is of a state that fosters greater social justice, transparency, freedom, and democracy. The goals are perhaps no different from those of many other disaffected and disenfranchised groups, but their strict adherence to Gandhian nonviolence is notable and a factor that taps into women's tendency to avoid the use of violence as a means of resolving disputes. (Anderlini 2007, 38)

These groups are characterized as being both feminist and pacifist.

Women's activist groups often rely upon their status as

mothers to further their causes because motherhood provides a

legitimate voice allowed by society's gender norms. The Madres de

Plaza de Mayo exemplify this very strategy. "By embracing and

strategically using the motherhood identity, however, they are

simultaneously reaching out widely to women and directly

challenging the moral authority of states that typically define themselves through social conservatism heavily dosed with militarism and traditional family values that uphold motherhood as the ultimate virtue" (Anderlini 2007, 39). By relying upon the role of mother, activist groups are thus coming from a more socially legitimate role and can be more effective. However, the impact of "seemingly innocuous and incongruous" activist groups is challenging to quantify (Anderlini 2007, 39). Because one measure of effectiveness is government reaction – often in the form of riot police, beatings, crackdowns, and arrests – it is more complex to measure the success of women's activist groups. Although women may face this type of violence, it may not be as visible or severe, due to their status as mothers. "The sudden emergence of mothers as the prime voices of dissent catches most dictatorial or militaristic regimes off guard" (Anderlini 2007, 39). This is key in disabling these regimes' violent and/or repressive responses. Women may also face less violent responses when acting under the auspices of religion (Mason 2005, 737). Regardless, women's activism does bring issues to public awareness, and their activism has played a key role in transforming the political arena and catalyzing public support (Anderlini 2007, 39).

Given the current patriarchal paradigm, it is not surprising that not every women's movement or activist group espouses feminist ideals. Rather, women's equality and feminist issues often take less precedence than achieving other common goals, such as ending war and conflict. Many women's activist groups are also more effective at achieving their aims when they work within existing traditional structures (Kaufman and Williams 2006, 29). As stated above, women's groups tend to be more easily accepted by the society when they call upon their roles as mothers and/or profess to act from religious motivations (Kaufman and Williams 2006, 18; Mason 2005, 737).

Women in Argentina used their status as mothers in order to wage nonviolent protest. "The Argentine Mothers of the Plaza de Mayo, who first gathered on April 30, 1977, in the plaza outside the presidential palace in Buenos Aires to protest their missing sons and daughters, are still celebrated, long after the military junta they opposed collapsed in 1983" (Anderlini 2007, 38). Beginning first as a group that stood outside the plaza, they soon took to walking around it as well. The women remained silent and met regularly on Thursdays. They did not hold signs or directly protest government action; rather, they wore white headscarves embroidered with the names of their sons and daughters. Here again, as is the case in other countries, women's activism is most effective when informed from and centered in traditionally accepted roles and institutions.

Women peacemakers in South Africa provide another example. "South African women ... were pivotal to the entire anti-apartheid movement and transition to peace" (Anderlini 2007, 42). Though underrepresented in local peace communities, women were instrumental as peace monitors. Not only did they enable access to communities, but they also fostered trust with these same communities. Again, women were successful when they drew upon their roles as mothers. According to one United Nations observer, men could be heard saying, "we need to show respect for our mothers" (Anderlini 2007, 42-43). When women involved in peacebuilding were interviewed, they, too, reiterated the need to work within certain structures and norms. "[W]omen participants' peacebuilding activities occurred primarily within local and regional grassroots women's groups and NGOs" (de la Ray and McKay 2006, 150). This lack of participation on an international level echoes other women's experience. "Workshop participants recognized that their peacebuilding initiatives were constrained through lack of power, voice, and recognition by self and others and that what they do differs from what men do to build peace" (de la Ray and McKay 2006, 149). Indeed, women's nonviolent activism exemplifies the inequalities addressed in feminist theory, and the two intertwined in a single movement may provide a successful organizational model for other social movements and activists.

Ethnography of Asheville Women in Black

Many methodologies exist for the study of social movements. For this study, I chose to take the perspectives outlined in movement-relevant theory. According to Bevington and Dixon in "Movement-relevant Theory; Rethinking Social Movement Scholarship and Activism," current social movement theory, particularly in the United States, "is in a quagmire" (Bevington and Dixon 2005, 185). Often, dominant social movement theory is not being read by movement participants nor is it useful. Movement-relevant theory, however, seeks to engage directly with movement participants and explore the theorizing being done by them. Movement-relevant theory promotes direct engagement for a specific reason: "One result of this engagement is better research as scholars develop deeper and more nuanced understandings of movements" (Bevington and Dixon 2005, 200). The research is no longer a detached, unbiased entity; rather, the researcher attempts to build a connection between herself and her research subjects. Thus, I chose to attend and participate in one of Asheville Women in Black's Friday vigils.

On October 2, 2009, I stood at a Women in Black vigil in Asheville, North Carolina. The day was windy and overcast; as a result, only five women, including myself, participated. One of the women brought her two young children, who ate dinner and played in the fountain as we stood. We stood where Asheville Women in Black has always stood – on the sidewalk in front of the Vance Park Monument; all of us were dressed in black. I was honored to be asked to hold one end of the banner, "Women in Black: A Silent Vigil Mourning Violence." As it was between five o'clock and six o'clock on a Friday evening, numerous cars passed by on Broadway Avenue. Though many drivers and passengers did not seem to notice or care, more than one honked when they saw us standing. At least two drivers flashed us a peace sign with their hands; we responded in kind. One young woman dressed in black stopped to ask for information about Women in Black. She stated that she saw the vigil every Friday and had finally decided to approach Women in Black. After a lengthy discussion with one of the more active members, she volunteered that she would be interested in standing with Women in Black on days allowed by her work schedule.

The vigil itself was not silent – my presence contributed to the discussion. I chose to individually interview each of the four women who attended the vigil, although they frequently paused to converse with each other for clarification. Each was asked basic, open-ended questions (see Appendix 1). Occasionally, I would ask additional questions for clarification, but, primarily, the women were allowed to speak as much or as little as they wished. The interviews were recorded using a hand-held Sansa Sandisk media player and recorder. As the interviews were recorded in a digital .wav format, they were easily uploaded to a computer hard drive for transcription. A few of the women were recorded more than one time, as they contributed additional information as the evening progressed. Afterward, we went for tea at the Green Sage to continue our discussion.

I also had the opportunity to interview three additional Asheville Women in Black, even though they were not able to attend the weekly Friday vigil on October 2, 2009. One of these interviews took place in person at an art gallery after the vigil – the specific woman was working at a Sister Cities exhibit that night. The other two interviews took place via email due to time and transportation constraints. All of the women were given my contact information in the form of my cell phone number and email address and were encouraged to contact me if they cared to share more information. Though initially the goal was to interview each women privately and individually, interviewing during the vigil and online yielded successful results. Not all of the women would describe themselves as outgoing; thus, allowing them to read and respond to the questions via email in writing facilitated participation with them. In addition, though the women were interviewed separately during the vigil, they were able to talk with each other while I conducted other interviews. This helped to facilitate greater reflection on the part of the participants, again leading to more detailed responses. Follow-up interviews were conducted a few month later, this time via email.

Asheville Women in Black Findings

In analyzing the interview and email transcripts from participating members of Asheville Women in Black, several themes emerged. Not every theme emerged, however, in every single woman's interview. Though several women shared similar views and motivations, Asheville Women in Black members were not in complete agreement on all issues and decisions. This is not surprising, given the diversity of the women participants – a completely unified voice would not be characteristic of this type of movement. Regardless, several of the themes are recognizable from scholars' research on other women's social movements.

Women Informing Other Women

One of the most common themes which emerged was that women who participated in vigils first heard of and became involved in Women in Black through word of mouth from other women. Pat spoke at length about the woman who brought her to Women in Black. "I began meeting strong women who had done all kinds of things during their life to make a huge difference ... and they just blow me away. They absolutely knock my socks off, make me feel

as though my life had been pretty much not counting for much..."
(Polansky 10.2.09). Dot, too, spoke of the woman who brought her
to Women in Black – Nancy (also another interviewee). Nancy had
been a student in Dot's graduate Nuclear Dilemma class and
mentioned to the class one week that she participated in Asheville
Women in Black vigils. According to Dot, it seemed like a good
idea to join (Sulock 10.2.09).

Clare, one of the founding members, was visited in prison
while serving a six-month sentence for nonviolent action. "A fellow
peace activist, Beth Trigg, visited and asked my support as she and
other women organized a weekly vigil to mourn the violence. When
I was released, I joined the women standing weekly at Vance
Monument" (Hanrahan 9.30.09). Anne, too, was brought to Women
in Black by the same woman as Clare. "Beth contacted me ... Beth
wrote an article calling for women ... to gather at Asheville's public
square, Pack Square, in a local paper, The Asheville Global
Report..." (Craig 9.26.09). Melissa was brought to Asheville
Women in Black by their constant presence at vigils, events, and
parades but was unable to attend initially due to her two young

children (Zenz 10.2.09). Clearly, word of mouth has proved to be the most effective means of communication.

Spirituality as Motivation

Three of the women cited spirituality as a source of inspiration and motivation to stand regularly. Pat met the woman who brought her to Asheville Women in Black at Jubilee Church in Asheville, where they are both members. She describes Jubilee as "...a conglomeration of all kinds of people, all kinds of beliefs, all kinds of faiths, or in some cases no faith, just whatever you want to do. It's just a bunch of folks getting together and experiencing the divine in all creation and in the Jubilee setting..." (Polansky 10.2.09). She also brought up sacred Hindu texts as a guide to living: "I certainly try to live my life by the virtues as listed in the *Bhagavad Gita*..." (Polansky 10.02.09). Dot spoke of the *Bible* as part of her inspiration, "Jesus said blessed are the peacemakers ... They shall be called the children of god" (Sulock 10.02.09). Anne cited the Bible as well, though she does not label herself as a Christian. "I am not a Christian, but I believe that this saying is attributed to Jesus: 'Where your treasure is, there will your heart be also.' I saw our treasure being sucked up by weapons of mass destruction and our leaders' hearts turning toward fear, threats and the use of violence" (Craig 9.28.09). Regardless of their spiritual beliefs, all the women felt a calling to do something active to bring awareness to the use of violence in Asheville and all over the world. This is not dissimilar to the notion of women acting under religious auspices in order to justify and legitimize their social activism.

Involvement with Other Causes and Actions

Nearly all of the women are also currently involved with other issues and actions. According to Dot, "The things that I do that are designed to save the world are usually connected with school" (Sulock 10.2.09). She cites her creation of "Reality Math," a mathematics program designed to introduce social issues into the curriculum, in addition to her graduate class, "The Nuclear Dilemma", and her Summer Nonproliferation Institute (Sulock 10.2.09). Clare states her actions are too numerous to list in their entirety. "I am conscientiously opposed to paying for war and a member of local and national tax resistance groups. As well as an associate member of Veterans for Peace ... and local chapter of War

Resisters League, Grandmothers for Peace, School of Americas Watch, ACLU, etc. etc." (Hanrahan 9.30.09).

Anne participates regularly in nonviolent actions. "In terms of 'civil disobedience,' I've 'crossed the line' twice at the School of the Americas demonstration/vigils at Ft. Benning, Georgia ... In terms of non-violent actions...too many to mention...many marches in Washington, D.C., rallies and vigils locally and in Raleigh, demonstrations at the nuclear weapons facilities in S.C. and Oak Ridge, Tennessee..." (Craig 9.26.09). Nancy works for three nonprofit organizations: Literacy Council, Sister Cities, and Habitat for Humanity. She lives in a cooperative community in Celo, North Carolina (since 1971) and was involved in Common Sense and the Nuclear Crossroads and Mobilization for Survival (Herman 10.2.09).

Both Pat and Melissa support animal rights. According to Pat, she is "extremely avid about animal rights ... I believe in what Gandhi said that until we can take good care of our animals, there's no hope for us as a species. Animals, probably, are my number one thing" (Polansky 10.2.09). Melissa describes herself as a vegan and runs a vegan business: Kidbean.com. "I'm a very big vegan activist" (Zenz 10.2.09). She is also involved in Carolina Animal Action,

Mercy for Animals, Asheville Vegetarian Group, NOW, PETA, and La Leche League (Zenz 10.2.09). This involvement with other causes is not surprising, as human beings and social issues are complex. It also places these women within Moyer's role of change agent; they seek to build coalitions among grassroots groups.

Concern for Children

Two of the women expressed that their concern for children was also a motivating factor in participating in both Women in Black and other causes and actions. Anne stated, "I spent my working life as teacher of young children and I started several schools. As a parent and teacher, I was very concerned about the world that our children would inherit. I didn't see it moving toward becoming a more just, peaceful, secure, healthy place and I felt a great responsibility to try to effect positive change to humanity in a better, more humane, sustainable, life promoting direction" (Craig 9.26.09). Melissa, who regularly brings her two small children to Friday vigils, echoed Anne. "I believe very much in nonviolent communication, conflict resolution. Having children, especially, I have that focus" (Zenz 10.2.09). She stated the importance of

bringing her children with her in order to "model" for them.
"They're here in bad weather and in good weather, often with food"
(Zenz 10.2.09). These women's statements correlate with the
literature, which states that women often use their status as mothers
to justify their social activism.

Belief in Community

Nearly all of the women stated that they see themselves as
part of a larger, global community, including not only human beings
but all of the planet also. Melissa refuses to carry products made by
companies that are not labor-friendly or ecofriendly. "I have a
section on my website called 'Why We Don't Carry,' so, if
companies don't do the things we think they should be doing, then
we call them out and our customers contact them, too" (Zenz
10.2.09). Clare describes herself in the following way: "I am a
member of the world community, concerned with issues of justice,
peace and defense of the Earth, and aware of my moral and legal
duty to dissent and to withdraw cooperation from the crimes of the
government" (Hanrahan 9.30.09). Anne listed as a concern
prompting her to action "...the violence we are doing to our Mother

Earth" (Craig 9.26.09). For Nancy, community is a main driving force in her life: "I believe in cooperatives" (Herman 10.2.09).

Pat, too, strongly believes in community, both local and international. "I would just like everyone to know that there is a very strong segment of women in Asheville who are extremely passionate about all kinds of causes, and this particular cause is nonviolence – not just violence against humans, but violence against our planet, violence against Mother Earth, the violence of rape in the Congo, the violence of domestic abuse, and, when you keep extrapolating on that, the violence of our negative thoughts, any negative energy that we put out there. It all serves for ill will all the way around" (Polansky 10.2.09). Dot spoke of her need to act in ways that "make a statement" and help "save the world" (Sulock 10.2.09).

Self-Identified as Activist

Despite their involvement in Women in Black as well as other actions and causes, the women did not necessarily see themselves as activists. Arida spoke of labels as problematic for her, "labeling oneself as something seems tricky to me" (Emrys 10.2.09).

Instead, she states that she will "Do what I can do when I can" and describes herself as "politically far left" (Emrys 10.2.09). Pat answered by comparing herself to others. "I certainly am not nearly an activist to the extent that many of the people here in Asheville that I know are, but I'm certainly much more of an activist now than I was when I was in the Dallas/Fort Worth area" (Polansky 10.2.09).

Some of the women, however, did identify with the label of activist. According to Dot, "I am also an activist because I'm a stubborn, outspoken person" (Sulock 10.2.09). Clare explicitly labeled herself an activist: "Yes. I have been a nonviolent activist for decades" (Hanrahan 9.30.09). Melissa defined herself as an activist, as well. "I'm a very big peace activist ... To me, I try to devote several hours every week to things I consider activist activities, which include writing letters to the newspapers and to businesses ... Because I have the business and I have the customers behind me, I have a little bit more clout than the average person" (Zenz 10.2.09). To Anne, activism is a part of citizenship. "I take my citizenship seriously. Thus I've been involved in may local community activities over the years in addition to addressing questions of foreign policy" (Craig 9.26.09). Nancy was less verbose when asked if she sees herself as an activist, "Yeah, I would" (Herman 10.2.09). As with any category applied to personal politics and actions, not everyone will agree on either the definition or the connotations of the term, in this case "activist."

Self-Identified as Peacemaker

Neither were the women unified in their response to the question of labeling themselves as peacemakers. According to Pat, "I work on peace in myself, I guess, and, as far as peace for the rest of the planet, well sure, I believe in taking care of Mother Earth and taking care of one another, and I definitely was totally opposed to the war" (Polansky 10.2.09). Melissa related her status as a peacemaker to her children. "I would, yes. I think one of the biggest things I do, too, is working with my children on conflict resolution" (Zenz 10.2.09). Dot related the label peacemaker to her spiritual beliefs. "Jesus said blessed are the peacemakers, so I'm happy to be a peacemaker" (Sulock 10.2.09). Nancy stated being a peacemaker as a goal. "I'd like to be a peacemaker, yes ... But I think it's difficult to be a peacemaker and to listen, particularly if you're ideological and if you have strong views" (Herman 10.2.09).

Arida stated that she has spent many years in meditation practice. "Trying to bring that so I'm dealing clearly with conflict, as clearly as I can – finding ways to be true to myself, feelings and things are going on and yet not doing it in a violent way" (Emrys 10.2.09). As with the category or label of "activist," the identification of oneself as a "peacemaker," is complicated. However, it seems as though "peacemaker" may be considered to be more desirable and have only positive attributes.

Self-Identified as Feminist

Although Women in Black is regularly referred to as a feminist organization and/or movement, not all of the women clearly identified themselves as feminists. Some of the women even stated their confusion regarding the term *feminist*. According to Arida, "I don't like labeling myself as a feminist because I don't even know quite what that means" (Emyrs 10.2.09). Nancy stated something similar. "I guess I'm a quasi-feminist. I don't really necessarily feel that. I think power corrupts, and I've seem women in positions of power who become corrupted. So, in that sense, I don't think that women could necessarily save the world. I'm probably more of a

Marxist than a feminist. I think I was more active as a feminist in the eighties" (Herman 10.2.09). Her response is not surprising; feminist scholars state that the label "feminist" itself as an interpretation of specific actions is problematic when those doing the actions may not identify as a "feminist" (Wright 2008, 381).

Some women did strongly identify with the term feminist. Dot stated, "Yes, I think of feminism as equal rights for women. Women should have equal rights. Not being a feminist would be silly" (Sulock 10.2.09). Anne's response was nearly identical to Dot's response. "I am a feminist in the sense of that radical idea that women are people! I do believe that if women across all segments of social and political life, had more 'power,' we'd live in a different and better world!" (Craig 9.26.09). Melissa was enthusiastic about her response to the term feminist. "Yes, absolutely. That I get from my mother. My mother's been very involved in politics, too ... She's always been on my case since I was a very small child to be independent, to be equal. She's a big supporter of the Equal Rights Amendment. I've grown up that way" (Zenz 10.02.09). Pat did not hesitate in her response, either. "I am, yes. I am extremely frustrated with males. I do think I'm probably, certainly lean towards the feminine side. I just feel as though the masculine energy has been the predominant one on this planet for way too long, and that, until we have a balance of male/female energies in all aspects of live, that there's little hope for peace and taking care of our planet – all those kinds of things" (Polansky 10.2.09). To these women, being labeled as a feminist is a positive attribute; although, that was not the case for all of the women.

Sense of Connection with International Women in Black

The women were varied in their knowledge of international groups of Women in Black, yet their impressions were positive. Pat stated she was not all that familiar with international Women in Black but was familiar with how it started. However, local issues and activism were more important to her. "If we could get the Palestinians and Jews to be able to live in peace in one location, that would be a huge step forward, but, at the same time, I need my neighborhood over in East Asheville to be able to live in peace when a black family moves in..." (Polansky 10.2.09). Melissa stated that she was not involved internationally with Women in Black; Asheville Women in Black is more applicable to her life. "I was really drawn to this because it is a peaceful vigil. We're not shouting in people's faces" (Zenz 10.2.09). Nancy stated that she was not really aware about what is currently happening with international Women in Black because she has not been abroad, but she was aware of their beginnings (Herman 10.2.09).

Other Asheville Women in Black were more knowledgeable about the beginnings of Women in Black internationally. According to Anne, when speaking about Clare and herself as well as another founding member of Asheville Women in Black, "All three of us were aware of Women in Black, its origins from the Mothers of the Plaza de Mayo in Argentina and Palestinian and Israeli women in Jerusalem vigiling as witness against disappearances and violence and injustice" (Craig 9.26.09). She also expressed the connection and honor she feels to be part of an international movement. "I think it's just great and amazing that women are using the tool of vigil to call attention to violence and injustice in their cities, nations and world. I felt connected to all women who vigil for a better society and world" (Craig 9.26.09). Arida commented on the feeling of connection, "Awesomely amazing – really feel that connection" (Emrys 10.2.09). According to Dot, "It's a really swell idea that someone founded it, so we can be a part of it, and I'm glad it's still going and happy to know that there's people all over the world doing this. It gives you some hope for the world" (Sulock 10.2.09). Clare expressed something similar. "I am honored to be associated with an international movement of women who stand in public and appropriate mourning for the daily violence of wars, occupations, and earth-killing policies of our governments" (Hanrahan 9.30.09). Thus the women do not see themselves as an isolated entity; rather, they sense a connection with a larger, global network of women activists and place themselves within the movement's historical context.

Influenced by Other Asheville Women in Black

In addition to feeling solidarity and connection with members of international Women in Black groups, some of the interview participants felt connected to and influenced by other members of Asheville Women in Black. Anne described another Asheville Women in Black member as "a sister vigiler" (Craig 9.26.09). Nancy mentioned more than once her admiration for other participants. "It's just been great meeting these women, and I wouldn't have gotten to know them ... For me, it's the standing day in and day out and the camaraderie with these particular women, who I think are great women, you know, strong women" (Herman 10.2.09). Pat was the most passionate in her response. "I have just met so many strong, dedicated, absolutely mindboggling women since I've been here. It makes me very proud to be a woman and gave me some reason to search into my own soul and reach down and see what I needed to be doing more for humanity and all of the suffering that goes on on our planet" (Polansky 10.2.09). Clearly, these women see themselves as part of a larger, perhaps global, community made up of primarily women.

Pride in Asheville Women in Black

One of the strongest themes to emerge from Asheville Women in Black interviews was the sense of pride the women felt. They truly believe that they are accomplishing something significant through their constant presence. Pat stated, "I would like for Asheville to just maybe have its conscience raised a bit when it sees us out here on Fridays ... I just think it's very good for the young women in the community, or anyone who sees us, to see us old greyheads out here, doing our thing. I think it may kind of help the younger women to see that there are people who are very passionate and that it's a good thing to stand for what you believe in" (Polansky 10.2.09). Melissa felt the same:

> We're just showing our presence, and it's a good reminder for people ... I think it's really important that someone is here almost every week. That we're a constant reminder to these people who drive by here every Friday. That we're still here. That somebody's still paying attention. Somebody is still outraged about the war and about violence all around the world, and it's just a reminder to them that somebody else is standing up and making a difference ... I think that that can instill in them a sense of confidence that they could do it, too ... It's important, that there's still violence that's happening all around the world. You might not see it in your life, but it is happening, and you need to do something about it. (Zenz 10.2.09)

Arida also spoke of the effectiveness of Women in Black; she believes they are bringing attention to the fact that "This is what violence does ... This is really what violence does – it's grief" (Emrys 10.2.09).

This pride was not only in drawing awareness to violence but also in the fact that Asheville Women in Black has stood for so long. Dot firmly announced, "We are absolutely persistent and consistent and proud of it" (Sulock 10.2.09). Clare said something very similar, "We prevailed and have continued to stand, uninterrupted from 2001 until present" (Hanrahan 10.2.09). Nancy confirmed this:

"It's important to know that we've been standing for, in one sense or

another, since 2001, and that's a long time and that we've really not

missed" (Herman 10.2.09). Anne gave specific dates:

> Our first vigil was held the first Friday of November, 2001.
> About 30 women attended. I was a committed vigiler for
> over seven years. I helped keep the vigil going by designing
> fliers, helping to create a web presence, participating in the
> creation of a banner, being responsible for bringing it to the
> weekly vigil, and writing articles about us. Sometimes, in
> very inclement weather I was the only vigiler for most of the
> hour. Amazingly, I was always joined by at least one other
> person by the end of the hour. (Craig 9.26.09)

Arida agreed, "So Women in Black just continues ... It's endured for

so long, through storms and snow and wind, and people coming and

going, disagreements and agreements, teas and no teas, cookies ...

and potlucks .... just kind of enduring ... in silence through lots of

changes" (Emrys 10.2.09).

Yet, some members expressed that they do not see Asheville

Women in Black's vigils are truly effective or instrumental in

changing attitudes or policies. Anne has since stopped attending,

stating, "I have stopped standing with Women in Black due to

personal feelings of futility and that the vigil had stopped being silent" (Craig 3.24.2010). Although she continues to participate in the vigils regularly, Dot echoed similar sentiments:

> Sadly WIB is most certainly overlooked and trivialized. In fact, WIB is trivial. A small number of women protesting or mourning in some public place regularly and with continuity is still trivial. Some nonviolent grassroots movements have "succeeded," in changing minds and changing laws, but these were huge movements: Ghandi, MLK, ... not too many in number (Sulock 11.2.2009).

Both Dot and Anne are clearly exhibiting Moyer's stage of "Perception of Failure." They perceive that Asheville Women in Black is not successful and are experiencing frustration and "burn-out."

Disagreement Regarding Nonviolent Practices

This is not to say that Asheville Women in Black have not had differences in theory and practice. For example, there was much disagreement regarding the effectiveness of an arrest, which occurred in 2003. Anne recounted the incident in a reverential manner.

> In March, 2003, our public square was closed to the public. Daily demonstrations were taking place protesting the impending invasion of Iraq and city officials believed that for public safety, the square would be closed and anti war protesters could

demonstrate at another location and pro war demonstrators could gather at yet another place. Women in Black moved to the designated antiwar location for daily vigils and after about four days of this, we decided to go back to the public square where we had been vigiling every Friday evening for the past sixteen months. It was a beautiful action for free speech and assembly. Over forty women attended the vigil holding photos of Iraqi civilians and our banner. When the police came and ordered us to disperse, the banner was handed to the ten women willing to risk arrest. The other women moved peacefully to the side streets bordering the square, singing softly. Many on-lookers gathered as the ten women held the banner aloft and the police informed each woman that they would be arrested if they didn't leave. Since our vigil is usually silent, as our spokesperson, I said that we would leave, as we always did, when our hour vigil was over. One by one the ten of us were arrested and taken off. As the last woman [was] arrested, I handed the folded banner to the arresting officer, who kindly handed it to a sister who approached from a side street to receive it. We were held for about five and a half hours in the Buncombe County   detention center. At our hearing in May, we pleaded innocent and I testified that the Constitution, which I held in my hand while 'on the stand,' clearly stated that we had the right to peaceably gather and that the Constitution was our 'permit.' We were found guilty of misdemeanor trespass and fined $150 each. The next week we held our vigil across the street from the still closed square. There were at least 50 women at that vigil. The following week, the barricades were removed from the square and we stood in our square again! (Craig 9.26.09).

This was the longest and most elaborate response Anne gave to any interview question. It seemed as if the arrest was a success story for Clare, as well. "In 2003, in response to the rising resistance to the wars and occupations of Iraq, and with clashing opinions on the street, the city of Asheville attempted to stifle dissent by closing the park to demonstrations. Women in Black were not deterred. We gathered in large numbers and stood, asserting our constitutional rights to assemble. Ten among the scores of women who gathered had agreed to risk arrest, if necessary, and were arrested" (Hanrahan 9.30.09).

Nancy, on the other hand, did not and still does not agree that the arrest action was one of the most important historical events of Asheville Women in Black.

> That action stemmed out of the anti-war sentiment ... The street was occupied day and night, and there were hecklers in front of the Art Museum, and there were the anti-war people in front of Pack Square. And the police put barricades up, basically, and told us, told the anti-war people that they needed to be in one place and the pro war people needed to be in another place. So, they put barricades up where we'd stand, and I personally felt like that was sort of a reasonable thing to do because it didn't matter to me whether we stood in one corner. It wasn't like we were being told we couldn't stand at all, and I could understand the reason for doing it. Also, most of the people who

were arrested had never stood with us before, and
they haven't stood with us since. I felt like it was
kind of taken over by, and people who had stood with
Women in Black since the beginning weren't
consulted before the action, so I didn't participate for
that reason. For me, that was not the high point. For
a lot of people, that was the high point of the whole
Women in Black, but, for me, it wasn't. For me, it
was just another kind of event (Herman 10.2.09).

Arida echoed a similar sentiment. "The rest of us just stood vigils

and stood outside the jail and supported them. Then there was some

tension because there were a lot of young people who wanted to

continue that kind of protest. But a lot of us just felt like that wasn't

really what Women in Black was about, and the people who were

protesting weren't even people who had been standing ever with

Women in Black. And they were kind of using it as a platform"

(Emrys 10.2.09). Nancy's closing sentiment echoed Arida. "I still

believe that, if we're going to have an action like that, then we

should discuss it with each other. We should all be consulted"

(Herman 10.2.09). This situation of disagreement surrounding the

public action leading to arrest demonstrates the lack of a single,

unified voice; Asheville Women in Black members, though all

aiming for the same goal, differ in their personal strategies and

politics.

Strategies for Overcoming Obstacles

Asheville Women in Black has endured other disagreements and obstacles, as well. A current frustration with Dot is the low numbers of vigilers on any given Friday. "We need more people to stand here. Once in a while there's only two, and we have three poles ... It's a little bit that things are better. It's better with Obama, and people don't see the need for statements against violence so much, but I still think it's important. The diehard persist" (Sulock 10.2.09). In fact, Dot believes that part of the reason Women in Black is still standing at all is due to the banner they hold during vigils. "I think the thing that is keeping us together at this time of diminishing bodies of Women in Black is this sign. Nancy Herman's wonderful sign adds this kind of consistency and solidarity to us and draws us all to Pack Place on Friday" (Sulock 10.2.09). In terms of the numbers of vigilers, Arida stated that "It kind of comes and goes" (Emrys 10.2.09). Nancy commented that

> There were a lot of people who aren't there anymore
> who were there in the very beginning ... There are just
> a few of us standing now, and I'm kind of wondering
> why that is. And it may be because, well, for one
> thing, the anti-war sentiment kind of faded away in
> Asheville. The Western Carolina Alliance folded,

and there isn't as much anti-war activism going on in Asheville right now (Herman 10.2.09).

Nancy also stated feeling a bit dissatisfied with the current format of Women in Black vigils. She is open to having vigilers hold signs and hand out literature pertaining to other issues, but this is an ongoing discussion among Women in Black. "I think one of the problems for me right now with Women in Black is that I'm feeling so frustrated with so many things that are going on ... I think some of us feel like we want to use the time to be a little bit more out there with certain issues ... It may be time to stir things up ... And it's true, I am feeling a need for a little more edge" (Herman 10.2.09). Arida, too, mentioned the current dilemma regarding carrying signs as well as early discussions about standing in silence versus talking (Emrys 10.2.09).

Nancy discussed the merits of a silent vigil versus one in which the women talk amongst themselves. "It's nice to be quiet ... For some people it's meditative, and we have these arguments about talking and not talking. It does say that we're a silent vigil and I've had people come by and go 'shh,' because we're sitting there yakking away, you know, and it is kind of embarrassing" (Herman

10.2.09). However, she also acknowledges that in regards to the other women vigilers, "...if I didn't talk to them I wouldn't get to know them" (Herman 10.2.09). Yet, Anne stated that she had stopped attending due to the lack of silence.

Other women told of more humorous events that had occurred during vigils. Dot recounted the time she thought she had lost the sign because in the beginning, a different individual was responsible for bringing the sign every Friday. "If you were going to be absent for some reason and you had the flag and the poles, it was really a dreadful thing. One time I thought I had lost the flag, and I was desperately searching for the flag all week long and nearly having a heart attack before I finally found the flag. I thought the world would end if I'd actually lost this beautiful flag" (Sulock 10.2.09). Nancy recalled that the sign had actually been misplaced twice in the past (Herman 10.2.09). This is not a worry anymore, as a business owner across the street from the vigiling location now stores the flag and the poles for Women in Black. They merely need to retrieve it each Friday before the vigil.

Dot also told of another encounter with a passersby, which occurred on Christmas Eve. "I remember Christmas Eve, when

Friday came on Christmas Eve, and some of us were standing here with this sign, and some people came by, and they said, 'This isn't a good thing to be doing Christmas Eve,' and I said, 'It's a really good thing to be doing Christmas Eve'" (Sulock 10.2.09). She also told of participating in a vigil during Bele Chere, a yearly city-wide festival in Asheville. "There you are. Everyone else is drinking beer and having a party. They're singing and dancing and you're standing there mourning violence silently. It's really strange" (Sulock 10.2.09). However, she was quite proud of these instances, "We do it" (Sulock 10.2.09).

Arida also shared some stories about past vigils and issues surrounding them, in particular a man of a different political persuasion. "And we had this guy, The Bush Man. We had this long dialogue about The Bush Man. It was like. I forget. It was sometime after Bush did something horrible, or maybe it was the election. It must have been the election. And he started to stand, he and his son, and it was like totally the opposite of signs of what we were doing ..." (Emrys 10.2.09). However, the women chose to respond according to the principles of nonviolence when faced with conflicts.

Non-hierarchical Organization

Arida was very impressed with the way Women in Black chose to respond to The Bush Man. "... it was how we all dealt with that. And we had this long email dialogue ... That was really wonderful" (Emrys 10.2.09). She was not the only woman who appreciated the nonhierarchical structure of Women in Black. According to Clare, "Women come and go as they can as we are a movement, not an organization" (Hanrahan 9.30.09). Nancy explicitly stated her belief in consensus and community and how that influenced her decision to become involved in Women in Black.

> What I liked about Women in Black was that it was a broad scope. It was women opposed to violence, and you could interpret that in any way. If your issue was domestic violence, you could approach it from that point of view ... I liked this, number one, because it was women, and, number two, it was an international organization ... And I also liked it because we didn't talk, and we didn't have meetings, and we didn't argue (Herman 10.2.09).

Nancy's statement exemplifies the participatory democratic nature of Asheville Women in Black.

Conclusion

Women in Black is a social movement according to Moyer's theory. Women in Black promotes participatory democracy by providing a role for anyone who wants to participate. Women participants attend as much or as little as they wish and are, for the most part, involved in the decision making process. Men are able to support, if not directly participate, by standing off to the side during a vigil, or, in the case of the male business owner, providing a storage place for the flag and poles. Even children are able to attend and participate through their visibility. Women in Black is also situated at the center of society and is based upon widely held universal values. They maintain a peaceful vigil and appeal to the common value of ending violence of all kinds. Women in Black does not seek to be perceived as a "fringe" group, and its intent is to calmly and consistently bring attention to the effects of violence. First and foremost, Women in Black is based upon the principles of active nonviolence. They stand in vigil, undertaking no radical or extreme actions. The Asheville group's banner is simple and non-offensive, stating "Women in Black: A Silent Vigil Mourning Violence." The participants are committed to nonviolence and, again in the case of the Asheville group, frown upon purposefully pursuing destructive acts of civil disobedience.

Moyer's stages of social movements can be seen in the history of Women in Black. It has clearly progressed through the fourth stage. In the case of Asheville Women in Black, it seems as though many of the women interviewed perceive their movement to be in the process of the fifth stage. Numbers of vigilers are dwindling, and frustration is prevalent; there is a perception of potential failure. Regardless, a few of the women's statements lead to the assessment that Asheville Women in Black may actually have progressed to the eighth, and final stage: continuing the struggle. They explain the low numbers as a function of improving conditions and do classify themselves as successful. These women were determined to continue to participate and were actively seeking ways to increase involvement and effectiveness. In addition, Women in Black fits into two of the categories outlined by West and Blumberg: they are concerned with nationalistic struggles as well as humanistic problems.

Due to the number and diversity of Women in Black groups, it is difficult to definitively categorize participants into Moyer's social movement participant roles. One role is overwhelming clear, however: that of the rebel. The women who participate in vigils are visible to the public and are partaking in an act of nonviolence. Women in Black participants are effective rebels, as they employ the tactics of civil disobedience and vigils to put the issue of violence in the public spotlight. Some women, however, may also be classified as change agents, as they are involved in other causes and seek to bridge various grassroots movements.

Women in Black also fits the description of Third Wave feminism. Participants disseminate information through word of mouth and the internet, and the movement itself is organized in a non-hierarchical way. In addition, as expressed by both International Women in Black and Asheville Women in Black, the diversity of women's experiences with violence is acknowledged. Women are not seen in essentialist terms. It is also fascinating that although some of the women call on their spirituality and/or their roles as mothers, the vast majority are standing just as women. "Women in Black ... have developed embodied feminist politics that not only bring the feminine body into view during wartime but also undermine the place of the good woman as the reproducer of the nation who mourns only for the lost soldiers of her people" (Cornell 2004, 313). In this way, they are exemplifying and expanding the roles of women further into the public sphere discussed in liberal feminist theory. Again, Women in Black is decidedly a Third Wave movement.

Women in Black stands as an important example of contemporary feminist active nonviolence. Its philosophy and methodology provide a blueprint for other feminist active nonviolent groups and movements; Women in Black's methodology and strategies are reproducible. By adding to a growing body of academic literature on Women in Black, this paper serves to document and explore in depth the reasons for Women in Black's continued activism as well as to provide a thorough explanation of Women in Black's methodologies and strategies. Indeed, other grassroots movements have already begun employing Women Black's vigil formal, most notably 350.org and MoveOn.org; both groups are currently active and have a strong online presence. It remains to be seen if history will consider Women in Black a successful social movement; world peace has yet to be achieved. One thing is for certain: Women in Black cannot be ignored; they have secured their place within a long history and tradition of

feminist activism and peacemaking.

References

Anderlini, Sanam Naraghi. 2007. *Women Building Peace: What They Do, Why It Matters*. London: Lynne Rienner Publishers, Inc.

Arneil, Barbara. 1999. *Politics & Feminism*. Oxford: Blackwell Publishers, Inc.

Asheville Women in Black. 2001. Women in Black to Vigil in Asheville. *Asheville Global Report*, no. 147 (Nov. 8 – 14), http://www.theglobalreport.org/issues/147/ (accessed August 4, 2009).

Baum, Dalit. 2006. Women in Black and Men in Pink: Protesting Against the Israeli Occupation. *Social Identities*, Vol. 12, No. 5 (September): 563 – 574.

Beckman, Peter and Francine D'Amico, eds. 1994. *Women, Gender, and World Politics: Perspectives, Policies, and Prospects*. Westport, CT: Bergin & Garvey.

Berkowitz, Sandra J. 2003. Can We Stand with You? Lessons from Women in Black for Global Feminist Activism. *Women and Language*, Vol. XXVI, No. 1: 94 – 99.

Bevington, Douglas and Chris Dixon. 2005. Movement-relevant Theory: Rethinking Social Movement Scholarship and Activism. *Social Movement Studies*, Vol. 4, No.3 (December): 185-208.

Cornell, Drucilla. 2004. The New Political Infamy and the Sacrilege of Feminism. *Metaphilosophy*, Vol. 35, No. 3 (April): 313 – 329.

Craig, Anne. 26 September 2009. Email message to author.

Craig, Anne. 24 March 2010. Email message to author.

De la Rey, Cheryl and Susan McKay. 2006. Peacebuilding as a Gendered Process. *Journal of Social Issues*, Vol. 62, No. 1: 141 – 153.

Emrys, Arida. 2 October 2009. Personal interview.

Gauneshpanchan, Zinthiya. 2009. Feminist Solidarity and the Cyber Crusade for Women's Activism: A Case Study of Women in Black. In *Cyber Conflict and Global Politics.* Athina Karatzogianni, ed. London: Routledge. 162 – 174.

Hanrahan, Clare. 30 September 2009. Email message to author.

Herman, Nancy. 2 October 2009. Personal interview.

Kaplan, Temma. 2004. *Taking Back the Streets: Women, Youth, and Direct Democracy*. Berkeley: University of California Press.

Kaufman, Joyce P. and Kristen P. Williams. 2006. Moving from the Private to the Public Sphere: Women Respond to War and Conflict. In the *Annual Meeting of the International Studies Association, San Diego, CA, 2006.*

Kostash, Myrna. 2003. Visible Silence: Women in Black in Edmonton. *Signs: Journal of Women in Culture and Society*, Vol. 29, No. 2: 591 – 593.

LeGates, Marlene. 2001. *In Their Time: A History of Feminism in Western Society*. New York: Routledge.

Mason, Christine. 2005. Women, Violence, and Nonviolent Resistance in East Timor. *Journal of Peace Research.* Vol. 42, No. 6: 737 – 749.

Moyer, Bill. 2001. *Doing Democracy: The MAP Model for Organizing Social Movements*. Canada: New Society Publishers.

Myers, Rebecca. 2001. Women-Only Prize Honors Peacemakers. *Christian Science Monitor*, Vol. 93, Issue 71 (8 March): 7.

Myers, JoAnne, Ph.D. Marist College. 16 November 2009. Email
message to author.

Polansky, Pat. 2 October 2009. Personal interview.

Schwebel, Milton. 2006. Realistic Empathy and Active
Nonviolence Confront Political Reality. *Journal of Social
Issues*, Vol. 62, No. 1: 191 – 208.

Sulock, Dot. 2 October 2009. Personal interview.

Sulock, Dot. 2 November 2009. Email message to author.

Svirsky, Gila. 2003. Local Coalitions, Global Partners: The
Women's Peace Movement in Israel and Beyond. *Signs:
Journal of Women in Culture and Society*, Vol. 29, No. 2:
543 – 550.

West, Guida and Rhoda Lois Blumberg. 1990. Reconstructing
Social Protest from a Feminist Perspective. In *Women and
Social Protest*. West and Blumberg, eds. New York: Oxford
University Press.

Women in Black. http://www.womeninblack.org/en/vigil.

Women in Black Asheville. http://www.main.nc.us/wib/.

Wright, Melissa. 2008. Gender and Geography: Knowledge and
  Activism Across the Intimately Global. *Progress in Human
  Geography*, Vol. 33, No. 3: 379 – 386.

Zenz, Melissa. 2 October 2009. Personal interview.

Appendix 1

Interview Questions:

1. Describe in detail your involvement in Asheville Women in Black.

2. What are your thoughts on the international component of Women in Black?

3. What factors, issues, or concerns drew you to Women in Black?

4. Are there other nonviolent actions you participate/d in?

5. Do you consider yourself a feminist, an activist, a peacemaker, or none of these? Explain.

6. What is the most important thing you want people to know about Asheville Women in Black?

7. Who were/are your major female influences? Explain.

8. Is/has Women in Black (Asheville and international) making/made any difference? Has the movement had any impact? Explain.

9. Why are you choosing to participate in a grassroots/activist movement? Is this more or less effective than working for change through official channels? Explain.

10. Is Women in Black successful? Relevant? Significant? None

of these? Explain.

11. Is it important that Women in Black is primarily a women-

only movement? Explain.